McClellan, Sherman and Grant

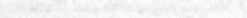

McClellan, Sherman and Grant

T. Harry Williams

Elephant Paperbacks

IVAN R. DEE, PUBLISHER, CHICAGO

McCLELLAN, SHERMAN AND GRANT. Copyright
© 1962 by Rutgers, The State University. This book
was originally published in 1962 and is here reprinted
by arrangement with Rutgers University Press.

First ELEPHANT PAPERBACK edition published
1991 by Ivan R. Dee, Inc., 1332 North Halsted
Street, Chicago 60622. Manufactured in the United
States of America and printed on acid-free paper.

Library of Congress Cataloging-in-Publication Data:
Williams, T. Harry (Thomas Harry), 1909–
McClellan, Sherman and Grant / T. Harry Williams.
— 1st Elephant paperback ed.
p. cm.
Reprint. Originally published: New Brunswick, N.J. :
Rutgers University Press, 1962. Originally published
in series: The Brown & Haley lectures.
Includes bibliographical references (p.).
ISBN 0-929587-70-7 (acid-free paper)
1. United States—History—Civil War, 1861–1865—
Biography.
2. Generals—United States—Biography.
3. McClellan, George Brinton, 1826–1885.
4. Sherman, William T. (William Tecumseh), 1820–
1891. 5. Grant, Ulysses S. (Ulysses Simpson),
1822–1885.
I. Title.
E467.W5   1991
973.7′0922—dc20   91-13761

Contents

McClellan, Sherman and Grant

A Note on Generalship

THE RATING OF Civil War generals is a favorite American pastime. Anyone with any interest in the most studied of our wars has at least one candidate for greatness. Every general who commanded a field army has his partisans, and even corps and cavalry leaders have their supporters who will contend that if their man had had an opportunity he would have emerged as the war's hero. The arguments swell across the land, rivaling in noise and fury the battles themselves. Curiously, in all the din hardly ever do the contestants attempt to set up any standards by which to meas-

3

ure generalship. If we are ever to understand anything about the subject of military leadership in
the Civil War, or in any war, we need to ask our-
selves some questions about the qualities that go
to make up generalship. Just how do you recog-
nize a great general? Exactly what is it that
makes a general great?

These are questions that cannot be answered
with objective finality. There can be no absolute
standards by which to determine greatness. Still
we should ask the questions, and we should attempt to identify some of the qualities that mark
the great general. It is probable that most people
make the business of evaluation too simple or too
complex. They make it too simple if they judge
only by results: it is possible for a general to win
a battle or campaign without himself being di-
rectly responsible for the outcome. They make it
too complex if they decide on the basis of education, experience, and technical skill: these are important but never determining factors. It is the
thesis of the following essays that the most vital
quality in a general is something all the great
commentators on war have called character. The
meaning of character in a general can be explained and developed, but it cannot be briefly
defined. The essays attempt to indicate the mean-

4

ing and importance of this hard-to-pin-down quality by tracing its influence on the career of certain Civil War generals.

Three generals are presented in these pages—
George B. McClellan, William T. Sherman, and
Ulysses S. Grant. They have been selected for
delineation for several reasons. They were prominent figures who played large parts in the war.
Each represents a particular and significant aspect
of leadership, and together they show a progression toward the final type of leadership that had
to be developed before the war could be won.
Most important, each one illustrates dramatically
the relation between character and generalship.
The personal material on them is fuller than for
other generals, and we can depict their temperaments and personalities and follow their course to
failure or success.

This venture into military analysis was prompted
by an invitation from the University of Puget
Sound to deliver the tenth Brown and Haley Lectures in the Social Studies and the Humanities.
The lectures were given in April, 1962, in sub-
stantially the form in which they are here presented. They are the product of both original re-
search and secondary reading and of years of
contemplation and repeated arguments with my

colleagues in blue and gray of the Civil War field. It is hoped that they will afford some insight into the always interesting and important problem of leadership in war, that they will perhaps indicate a new and rewarding approach. There is no hope that they will still the arguments over the generals of the Civil War.

Now I must express my gratitude to many gracious people at the University of Puget Sound who made my visit there a week of delight—President R. Franklin Thompson, Professor Lyle S. Shelmidine, Dean John D. Regester, and more representatives of the faculty than I can name here; and every member of the unfailingly interesting Haley family. But most of all, I enjoyed the students and the people who made up the audiences. They were so responsive that each lecture became an increasing joy to deliver.

Baton Rouge, Louisiana   T. HARRY WILLIAMS
April, 1962

George Brinton McClellan

---◆◆►---

In the tense days of 1861, when McClellan seemed like the savior of the Union, the press and the public called him the "Little Napoleon." His soldiers of the Army of the Potomac, the superb fighting body he created, called him "Little Mac." Soon many of those civilians who had hailed him most adoringly would denounce him as an imbecile, and some would even hint he was a traitor. But the soldiers loved George Brinton McClellan to the last or at least up to the election of 1864, when he took on a new identity as a politician. At Gettysburg the rumor ran through the ranks that

McClellan had been restored to command, and officers let it run, knowing the belief would lift the men to higher endeavors. There was something special about this man for the common soldiers. Whenever he appeared, in victory or in defeat, on the field or in the camp, they dropped anything they were doing to cheer and throw their caps in the air and press close to him. It was said that McClellan was the only general who by merely riding up could induce enlisted men to leave their breakfasts and follow him.

This adulation was not aroused simply by his presence, although that was inspiring and martial in itself. He was a man of five feet eight inches, with tremendous shoulders and a chest that measured forty-five inches around. Dark-auburn hair and a shapely head crowned a face of regular features. He looked in 1861 even more youthful than his thirty-five years but at the same time maturely confident and competent. He sat firm and erect in the saddle, the seeming embodiment of all the soldierly virtues. There were other generals who cut as fine a figure and sat a horse as well, but although some of them could stir their troops to enthusiasm and devotion, nobody else could call up the emotions that McClellan did. In part it was that he had the quality called charism, which the great political mass leaders have possessed, the power to excite people merely by appearing before them. And in part it was that he identified himself with the men, imparting to them in some undefinable way that he cared greatly for them and would watch over them, and they sensed this and responded by loving him. Perhaps both he and they between them created something like a father image that neither could let go. This relationship between McClellan and his men, his love affair with the army in the mass, one might say, was one of his strengths and also one of his fatal weaknesses. He loved his men so much he could not bear to sacrifice them in battle.

His strengths and weaknesses, his qualities as a general, are and long have been a subject of dispute between historians and students of the war. In fact, there is no figure of the conflict who is so much a center of controversy as McClellan. His reputation has undergone several cycles of evaluation and re-evaluation. The most recent judgment is that he was not a good general, was even a bad one, although there are still some who contend that he was a great captain who, if he had not been thwarted by forces beyond his control, would have won the war for the Union much sooner than it was won. Even his severest critics concede that he had administrative ability and was an excellent trainer of troops. Indeed, the consensus is that in such matters as training and organization McClellan ranks with the best. But even on this one point of seeming agreement there is discord. McClellan's most inveterate critic, the late Kenneth P. Williams, concluded: "Surely the verdict must be: McClellan was not a real general. McClellan was not even a disciplined, truthful soldier. McClellan was merely an attractive but vain and unstable man, with considerable military knowledge, who sat a horse well and wanted to be President." Over the years the McClellan debate has run on, and it will run for more years. McClellan, both as a man and as a soldier, is so complex and so converse and so bewilderingly one thing and then another that we can never be sure which aspect of him is real. Studying McClellan is like studying several men or several soldiers in one.

He was never badly beaten in battle or driven from the field in a rout. Yet he never won a decisive victory or drove an enemy. He never risked the lives of his men needlessly, and he shrank from bloodshed. Yet he commanded in the bloodiest single day of the war. He is always considered as a cautious leader with a defensive psychosis. Yet his two largest operations were offensive in concept, and in both he inflicted heavy losses on the foe. At the beginning of the battle of the Seven Days he lost his nerve and seemed to suffer a complete collapse. But almost immediately he conducted the most skilled fighting withdrawal of the war. He created opportunities for victory and then refused to exploit them. On three occasions he had it in his power to deliver damaging and perhaps killing blows at his adversary—after the first meeting of the Seven Days, after Malvern Hill, and, over all, at Antietam—but at the critical moment he drew back his hand.

McClellan could be at once, in the same day or even the same hour, noble and self-seeking, generous and petty. He intrigued hard to have General Scott removed as his superior. But when he saw Scott depart Washington at the railway station, he dissolved in tears of pity for the old man's fate—and in tears of self-pity for what might be his own fate. In anything he wrote, whether it was a private letter or an official communication, he could exhibit from sentence to sentence the most arrant arrogance or the most becoming humility and move back and forth from the highest elation to the deepest pessimism.

The qualities that go to make up a general are

several: his native intelligence, his education and experience, his technical skills, and his judgment in picking men to assist him. Each is important, and the great captain has to possess all or most of them in one degree or another. But all of them together are not enough to constitute greatness if another element is lacking. The final and essential quality is something that the most acute students of war, including some of the most successful practitioners of the art, have called "character." What they mean is somewhat difficult to delineate because it concerns an ingredient of the human spirit or a component of the nature of a man. It might be defined most simply, although not with complete accuracy, as moral courage or plain nerve. It is what enables a commander to dominate any situation that may develop, to attain a psychological initiative over his adversary while suppressing his own fears and doubts, to surmount what Clausewitz in an apt phrase called the "inertia of war."

In the last analysis, then, the true measurement of a general will be his temperament. He may display any number of professional abilities and yet fail in his profession if he does not possess the temperament for command. Some soldiers have this temperament and some do not. Why this should be so is not for the historian to say. The reasons lie in realms beyond his ken and, because of the imperfect data of the past, beyond the comprehension of any analyst. It is possible, however, to discover and describe the temperaments of many soldiers. The process is rewarding, because it tells us as nothing else can why some generals met the fate they did—why some rose to greatness and others sank to failure. The task of dissection is comparatively easy with McClellan. He left abundant private materials, especially in the form of letters to his wife. Of these missives it has been said that it was remarkable that he ever wrote them in the first place and even more remarkable that he published them in his autobiography for all the world to see.

There was nothing in McClellan's life or person before the war to suggest the dualism and the doubts that would mark him as a soldier. His career up to 1861 was an unbroken success story. Born in Philadelphia of well-to-do parents, he enjoyed a good preparatory education and then entered the Military Academy at West Point. There he compiled a brilliant record and graduated second in his class. His army service indicated a promising future. He won distinction as a junior officer in the Mexican War and thereafter rose

rapidly in the estimation of his superiors. Assigned to ever more important duties, he was sent
to Europe as a member of a commission to study
and report on the latest developments in war. In
Europe he was able to observe operations in the
Crimean War, thus supplementing with firsthand
knowledge his wide reading in several languages
on strategic theory.

Although he was obviously tagged for advance-
ment, McClellan resigned his commission in 1857
to enter the more lucrative world of business. He
was an accomplished engineer and became a high
official in two of the largest railroad companies in
the country. On the eve of the war he was living
in Cincinnati and enjoying his wealth and social
position. He considered himself to be, as he was,
a gentleman of culture and background: an
American aristocrat. He knew many things—what
Napoleon and Jomini had written about how to
plan a battle, what the textbooks said about how
to conduct a siege—and some of his learning
would be useful to him in the war. The things he
did not know were surprising and would be fatal.
He knew almost nothing about his country and
the pulsing currents that had brought it to civil
conflict or about people outside his own small
and genteel circle. As far as the records show, he

had never experienced a moment of strain or crisis or inner doubt.

When hostilities began, McClellan offered his services to Ohio and was commissioned a major general of volunteers. Almost immediately the government in Washington named him to the same rank in the United States army and assigned him to an important mission. Just over the Ohio River lay western Virginia, a region of active Union sympathies and potential strategic value. The Federal government wanted to possess it, and in the summer of 1861 McClellan directed a campaign that secured a firm and broad foothold. There is some question as to whether McClellan or his subordinates were responsible for the victories achieved, but as the commander he received the credit from the public and the government. The acclaim for him was tremendous and out of proportion to his deeds. But successful Northern generals were so rare at the moment as to be curiosities, and the young soldier out in the mountains seemed a veritable hero, an emerging genius.

Lincoln, looking around for a general to take over the Union forces after the debacle of Bull Run, naturally thought first of McClellan and summoned him to Washington. McClellan came on immediately and plunged with feverish energy into the job of training the masses of troops that the government placed at his disposal, the masses that he shaped into the fine instrument to be known as the Army of the Potomac. He was looked on as a savior, and he accepted the role. It was one that he was not ready for and that should not have been thrust upon him. With small experience in handling men in numbers, he was abruptly placed in command of the largest army yet assembled in America. With slim experience in field command, he was expected to organize this host and crush the rebellion in one grand movement. Everything about the situation was unreal—the public's image of McClellan, the government's image of what he could accomplish, and, most unreal and most tragic of all, McClellan's image of himself. This man who had never been tested or tempered by the realities of life saw nothing strange in what was happening. He was not surprised. He thought the McClellan of the image was real.

As McClellan entered western Virginia and when he left there for Washington, he wrote his wife detailed accounts of his movements and his most inner thoughts. These letters, extraordinary in their revelatory character, are enough in themselves to provide the basis for a personality analysis. Quotations from them foreshadow almost precisely the kind of general McClellan would be. In West Virginia: "At every station where we stopped crowds had assembled to see the 'young general.' . . . I could hear them say, 'He is our own general.' . . . I hope to thrash the infamous scamps before a week is over. All I fear is that I won't catch them. . . . Well, it is a proud and glorious thing to see a whole people here, looking up to me as their deliverer from tyranny. . . . I realize now the dreadful responsibility on me— the lives of my men, the reputation of the country and the success of our cause. . . . I shall feel my way and be very cautious."

And when he arrived in Washington: "I find myself in a new and strange position here . . . all deferring to me. By some strange operation of magic I seem to have become the power of the land. . . . When I was in the Senate chamber to-day and saw those old men flocking around me; when I afterwards stood in the library . . . and saw the crowd gathering around to stare at me, I began to feel how great the task committed to me . . . who would have thought, when we were married, that I should so soon be called upon to save my country? . . . I shall carry this thing *engrand* and crush the rebels in one campaign."

On the necessity for getting rid of General Scott, his superior, and on hints that he should be a dictator: "I have no choice. The people call on me to save the country. I must save it, and cannot respect anything that is in the way. . . . I have no such aspirations. I would cheerfully take the dictatorship and agree to lay down my life when the country is saved."

On the developing danger from the enemy and the refusal of the politicians to see his problems: "I am here in a terrible place: the enemy have from three to four times my force. . . . I can't tell you how disgusted I am becoming with these wretched politicians. . . . I have a set of men to deal with unscrupulous and false; if possible they will throw whatever blame there is on my shoulders . . . I can't move without more means."

On his mission to save the country despite such incompetents and tricksters as Lincoln: "I did not seek it. It was thrust upon me. I was called to it; my previous life seems to have been unwittingly directed to this great end . . . God can accomplish the greatest results with the weakest instruments. . . . He could not have placed me here for nothing."

Here in these early letters written before he ever came to grips with any big problem or with the enemy are most of the ingredients of George B. McClellan—a fascination with people in the mass but at a proper distance; a conviction that these people who stare at him so intently are thinking that only he can save them; a determination to save those who so adore him, whether they be civilians or soldiers; a rising doubt that he may not be able to accomplish his purpose because the enemy, who at first appeared so contemptible, was suddenly increasing in numbers; and a gnawing fear that men on his own side, men in high places, are for mysterious but sinister reasons conspiring to overthrow him.

In these letters that said so much about people in crowds or armies there was, too, an utter inability to estimate people as individuals. Nowhere was this more apparent than in the references to McClellan's immediate civilian superior, Abraham Lincoln. At McClellan's first acquaintance with Lincoln he viewed the President as well-meaning and honest but a bumpkin, the kind of man whom democracy often elevated to high office and who had to be guided by their betters. McClellan graciously tried to work with Lincoln and other like fellows in the civil government, but their dull incapacity wore out his patience. Gradually the picture of Lincoln in the letters changed, from merely an amusing nuisance to "the original Gorilla" who was a disgrace to the nation. And then McClellan perceived something else. These politicians might be dull, but they were cunning. They were, in fact, the very men who were conspiring to destroy him, and if Lincoln was not one of them, he was letting himself be used by them.

All the evaluations of McClellan start from a military basis. They assume that because he was a general he has to be measured in a purely military framework. Those that are favorable point to his skill in organization and administration and to the superb morale of his army, and argue that if he had not been thwarted by political interference he would have won the war. Those that are critical emphasize his excessive caution, his habitual exaggeration of the size of the enemy forces, his devotion to traditional practices of warfare, his failure to establish trustful relations with Lincoln, and contend that he did not possess the qualities for field command.

Some of these judgments on both sides are valid, and obviously some military standards have to be used in assessing McClellan or any soldier.

For example, no really objective observer can deny that McClellan was a fine trainer of troops. The Army of the Potomac was his creation, and he was able to make it into what is was because he was a professional at this kind of thing, because he had the technical know-how and the sheer energy to whip a mass of green recruits into a disciplined army. It is also true that his whole concept of war and strategy was a product of his military education. That concept, drawn from his courses at the Military Academy and from his reading of the works of the French military writers, was eighteenth century in origin and outlook. It envisioned war as a limited and leisurely exercise, to be conducted by professionals as something like a game and to be played on a strategic chessboard with little loss of life.

Most of the West Point generals, coming from the same background, had at first the same philosophy; they professed to believe that by maneuver alone a campaign could be won without ever fighting a battle. But it is safe to say that no other general accepted the theory so completely as McClellan did nor let himself be so affected personally when it was proved wrong. He was wholly unnerved when he saw the aftermath of his first battle, men actually dead and wounded, and wailed to his wife: "I am tired of the sickening sight of the battle-field, with its mangled corpses and poor suffering wounded! Victory has no charms for me when purchased at such cost. . . . Every poor fellow that is killed or wounded almost haunts me!" Two of his victories did charm him, his captures of Manassas and Yorktown, both occupied after the enemy had evacuated them. Of Manassas he wrote with complete seriousness: "History will, when I am in my grave, record it as the brightest passage of my life, that I accomplished so much at so small a loss."

History would not, of course, record it that way at all, would, if giving it any attention, merely note that it was a meaningless operation that had no important effect on the course of events. And historians have wondered how McClellan could make such a statement and others like it, how he could so grossly misrepresent a situation. The crux of the problem is that he did not think he was misrepresenting. He actually believed that Manassas and Yorktown were great victories and that history would so define them.

This inability to see things as they were is the key to the whole McClellan problem. He can never be understood if viewed only in a military context. Other generals came from the same background and had the same military notions as he, but none of them acted quite as McClellan did. He is so different from all the others as to be unique and can be explained only in terms of his personality or psychology. When all the good things that can be credited to McClellan are written down, when all his possible abilities are listed, one damning indictment still stands out. He did not have the temperament for command. The vital element that was lacking, whose absence negated all his virtues, was a sense of realism. He could not see anything—a military situation, a battle, or even life itself—as it actually was. He saw everything as he wanted it to be. Almost literally he lived in a world of make-believe that he peopled with a few friends and with many enemies who were bent on destroying him. The tragedy of it all was that he insisted his imaginary world was real. All analyses of McClellan will have to come in the end to this one quality that explains all the aspects of his generalship—his own peculiar vision of himself and the scenes around him.

McClellan began to demonstrate his inability to see things real or, conversely, his ability to see them unreal almost immediately after coming to Washington. The government was assembling a huge force around the capital, and McClellan de-

voted the late summer and fall months to training
the mass of recruits. The job had to be done and
he did it well, but he overdid it. He stretched the
training period out beyond any reasonable limit
and went into the winter without undertaking a
campaign. On several occasions he indicated that
he was ready to move, but at the last minute he
found excuses not to—the enemy had been rein-
forced, he needed more men, the weather and
roads were unfavorable.

Lincoln hoped that McClellan would be able to
strike and end the war with one blow. Lincoln's
notion that a single thrust would finish the Confederacy has been criticized by historians as being naïve and as expecting too much of McClellan. It was both of these, but it was, curiously, the
exact objective McClellan intended to accomplish.
He meant to advance with an army so overwhelming that he would be irresistible. His most frequently expressed reason for not advancing was
that he had not yet forged such an invincible aggregation: "I feel however that the issue of this
struggle is to be decided by the next great battle,
& that I owe it to my country & myself not to advance until I have reasonable chances in my favor.
. . . I will pay no attention to popular clamor.

*Williams
agrees w/ on
archer
agrees w/
wm*

. . . When the blow *is* struck it will be heavy, rapid & decisive."

The popular clamor that McClellan referred to was real. All over the North people were asking why the magnificent Army of the Potomac remained idle. But Lincoln was willing to sustain his young general in his request for more time. The President did, however, again and again urge McClellan to undertake some kind of movement, even a minor one—a probe at the Confederate lines lying only some twenty miles south of Washington, an attempt to break the enemy blockade of the Potomac, anything that would convince the public McClellan meant business and would ultimately strike a major blow.

In these interviews Lincoln tried to impress on McClellan one of the great truths of war, especially of war waged by a democracy: that sometimes military movements have to be launched for political objectives, in this case, to sustain the Northern will to continue the war. What Lincoln was saying, with a special application to McClellan, was that unless a general did something to promise future victory, the people on whose support the war effort depended might become discouraged and give up the whole game. That is,

*political
objectives
+
Northern
will*

27

without some action now there would be none later, no armies for McClellan or any general to lead, and no war. The relation between policy and war is one of the vital facts of war, especially of modern and democratic war. Lincoln knew it, just as in a later and greater war Roosevelt and Churchill would know it.

McClellan dismissed these suggestions of his civilian superior. It is probable that he did not know what Lincoln was talking about. He simply had no notion of the relation between war and politics, no realization of the political objective of war. His obtuseness was in part the result of his education in traditional methods of warfare. Like many professional soldiers on both sides, he conceived of war literally as a game conducted by experts off in a corner, so to speak, and separated from society. When an expert had his pieces all ready he moved, but not before. Therefore to McClellan the ideas of any civilian, whether Lincoln or a lesser individual, were irrelevant—the civilians had no business interfering with the game.

Actually the civilians were going to interfere a great deal in this particular game and increasingly in every conflict after it. The Civil War, the first of the modern wars, saw the beginning of what would be one of the great changes in warfare, the emergence of the civilian as a factor in strategic planning. Whether the soldier liked it or not, the civilian was coming into war to stay, and this was something every soldier had to adapt to. In the Civil War the civilians were going to impress on the generals, among other things, that the conflict was being fought for important policy objectives and that the military was to achieve these ends quickly and ruthlessly. The stakes were too high to permit a leisured movement of the pieces.

Most of the West Point generals had at the beginning the same unpolitical concept of war as McClellan. Some never outgrew it and some did. It might be expected that McClellan, who was undeniably intelligent and who had had experience in the world of the civilian, would be among those who would realize the new power structure and most easily adapt to it. But the opposite is true. McClellan never grasped the political character of the war, he never accepted the civilian as a factor in the war. He did not even seem to comprehend that the political-civilian branch of the government was supposed to have a significant part in determining how the war should be conducted. He could not comprehend because his mental picture of the situation, in fact, of his country, was distorted and characteristically unreal. He was not consciously opposed to democracy but certainly he did not understand it. In temperament and taste he was an aristocrat. All his associations outside the army had been with men of wealth, and he and his closest intimates in the army believed that these capitalists controlled, or should control, the government.

To McClellan and his inner circle politicians were not the representatives of the people, but low fellows who unfortunately were in a position to interfere with gentlemen and generals. Here were the generals trying to save the country, exclaimed Fitz John Porter, one of the McClellan group, and their labors were "upset" by the "political coward" in the White House. "We can save the country," McClellan assured another general, "if wicked politicians don't prevent us." Actually McClellan mingled a great deal with politicians, particularly those in the Democratic camp, and continually instructed those of both parties on matters of policy. Paradoxically, he had a strong sense of realism on many political issues, and on the great issue of slavery he and Lincoln were not far apart, both being gradual emancipationists. But McClellan thought that the question of the wartime disposal of slavery should be subordinated to military requirements. He had everything reversed. Instead of strategy being an instrument to accomplish national policy, policy was to serve strategy. And George B. McClellan rather than Abraham Lincoln should determine the main outlines of both.

At first McClellan acted as commander of the Army of the Potomac, regarded as the most important Northern field army, and as a kind of unofficial adviser to the President. Then when old General Scott retired, McClellan became also general in chief of all armies, holding this post from November of 1861 to April of 1862. Thus for a period he occupied two large command positions, and in both capacities he was expected to deal with matters of large strategy, strategy for the armies on all fronts and for his own army in the Eastern theater.

Soon after McClellan came to Washington, Lincoln, as if to test his ability to deal with broad strategy, asked him to prepare a plan of general operations to crush the Confederacy. McClellan came up with one of the most astonishing official papers of the war. In it he proposed to gather a host of 273,000 men—why it had to be this odd number he never explained—in the Eastern theater. Under his command it would sail in transports down the Atlantic coast and successively seize all the key cities from Richmond to New Orleans, whereupon the Confederates, although their armies would not be destroyed, would submissively give up the war. It was a pretty paper exercise, and it had no relevance at all to anything in the existing condition of affairs. The government could not have assembled that many men or ships, and even if it could it should not have concentrated that much power in one theater at the expense of others equally important. McClellan's plan was neat and logical and took account of everything but reality.

As far as the records show, Lincoln never asked McClellan to act on the plan and McClellan never pressed for its adoption. Both must have been relieved at the outcome, Lincoln because the proposal was shelved and McClellan because he could now devote himself to what interested him most, theater strategy for his own army. McClellan had no talent for grand strategy. He could not, as his plan revealed, really conceive of operations in other theaters except as auxiliary support to his own movements. In the winter of 1861-62 he turned over in his mind ways of getting at the Confederate capital of Richmond. He finally hit on a plan which he divulged to a few intimates and eventually even to the President. At the time, McClellan's army was stretched around Washington and a Confederate army estimated by McClellan to number 100,000 (actually it was 50,-000) lay at Manassas, approximately thirty miles to the south. McClellan proposed to advance on Richmond along one of the waterways from the east, the Rappahannock River, his first choice, or the York or the James. To make such a move, his own army would have to leave Washington on transports, sail down the Potomac and the coast, land at a secure base, and push inland.

The plan, as McClellan outlined it, offered solid advantages. The land distance the army would have to traverse was shorter by half than the overland route from Washington. The terrain was supposed to be less defensible, although this was something of which McClellan had convinced himself without adequate exploration. The army would move on a secure line of water communications with naval support and with one or both of its flanks protected by the rivers. Above all, the plan promised a quick and decisive success, and McClellan was completely ecstatic about it.

It was a good plan. It had most of the merits proclaimed by its author. If a student at West Point had worked it out as an exercise for a theoretical war, he would have been awarded an A plus. There was only one fault with it. Like his plan of grand strategy, it ignored every reality in the human and political structure of which McClellan was a part. It was certain to arouse the distrust and opposition of every one of his civilian superiors from Lincoln on down. McClellan could not make his move without uncovering Washington, yet he proposed to make it with an enemy army that he himself said was 100,000 strong poised only a short distance from the seat of government. This was the feature of the plan that disturbed Lincoln, that led him to raise strong objections to its execution. Patiently and with some condescension McClellan explained why there would be no danger—he would leave an adequate defensive force behind him, and his move would compel the Confederates to leave their present position and shift to meet him.

Historical supporters of McClellan argue in the same spirit and logic—there was no need for the not-too-bright Lincoln to be alarmed. And from the viewpoint of pure theory McClellan was perfectly right, and his advocates are right. Washington was in small danger. But McClellan was not acting in a theoretical situation. He was dealing with real people who had real fears. Lincoln, as the political chief of the nation, was properly sensitive about the safety of the capital, whose fall would be fatal, leading among other things to possible European intervention in the war.

No political leader would easily agree to expose the nerve center of his country in reliance on the outcome of a battle to be fought at a distance by a general who had not as yet proved himself in the field. If McClellan wanted to induce acceptance of his plan he had to give the government a feeling of security about it. This he failed to do, largely because he could not bring himself to take his civilian superiors into his full confidence. But he should not have urged the plan at all after Lincoln's opposition was apparent. No general can succeed without the trust of his government, and McClellan lost that trust by insisting on his plan and his alone. When the Confederate army by a retrograde movement made it impossible for him to operate on the Rappahannock, he still did not abandon his purpose—he had to move on a waterway, and he would now use the York or the James. McClellan should have offered to prepare another plan or to resign. He won Lincoln's reluctant assent to his movement, but he never enjoyed the President's full support. When McClellan evaded, to put it mildly, his promise to leave enough troops around Washington to make the city safe, Lincoln did not hesitate to order a whole corps from the army retained near the city.

McClellan could never understand why anybody should object to his scheme. He could not understand because he did not understand the men and the scenes around them, did not see them as they really were. It was said above that McClellan was not acting in a theoretical situation. But in a sense he was. He was moving in the world of his own mind, that world where all things were as he wanted them to be.

In the spring of 1862 McClellan took his army to the York-James line to begin his campaign against Richmond. He was now approaching the ultimate and greatest test of a field commander, the moment when he would feel the stress of actual combat, when the inertia of war would come to rest on his single will. He would fail in field command, as surely as he had as a strategist and for the same reason. He could not see anything about a battle, its preliminaries, its course, its outcome, as it really was. He saw everything through the lenses of his mind, as it was supposed to be. The most frequent criticisms of McClellan are that he was too cautious, that he was not aggressive enough, that he was, in the words of one critic, constitutionally timid. As he came to a battle, an apprehensive anxiety seemed to grip him, a nervous oppression to settle on him. Yet McClellan did not regard himself as cautious or hesitant. On the contrary, he thought he was a bold and aggressive soldier. And he was not cautious or timid or any of the other things the critics have charged. He did not shrink from engaging in battle or draw back his hand after engaging because he was afraid. It was bigger than that. He acted as he did because he saw in front of him awesome dangers, awesome aggregations of enemies, and he had to protect his men from destruction. If these dangers were not real, they were real to McClellan and they were always present.

The great danger appeared immediately after he arrived in Virginia. It never left and, indeed, grew constantly greater. The Confederates had more men than he, and no matter how many reinforcements he received they managed in some way to get still more. His estimates of the size of the opposing army were fantastic. It is true that he was served by a bad intelligence organization. But he had selected it, and he wanted to believe what he heard. In early April, when the Confederates had 50,000 men, he put them at 100,-000. When he began operations at Yorktown, they

still were 50,000, but he evaluated them at 100,-
000 or 120,000. In late June, when he was near
Richmond and just before they launched a coun-
terattack on him, they had brought their force up
to 86,000. He judged them to be 180,000, and
when the attack struck he upped the figure to
200,000. Everything that McClellan did in the
decisive engagement that followed, the battle of
the Seven Days, was based on the assumption
that the enemy outnumbered him two to one. The
situation was not what it was in actuality, but
what it was in McClellan's mind. It was the supreme example of his gift for fantasy.

McClellan failed in his Virginia campaign. His
army was by Lincoln's order brought back near
Washington to be united with one under John
Pope for a new movement. When the Confederates
hit Pope before all of McClellan's troops had come
up, the government transferred that part of the
army on the scene to Pope. Pope fought and lost
the battle of Second Bull Run and was relieved
from command.

McClellan took over the control of all the forces
around Washington, the beaten soldiers receiving
him with an extravagant display of affection. He
marched the army out to meet Lee's invasion of
Maryland. Learning by the accident of some cap-

tured orders that the Confederate army was divided, he pushed ahead with what was for him precipitate speed. At South Mountain he dislodged a Confederate force seeking to delay him while Lee brought his units together and with his usual inability to see things real he told his wife this small action was one of the greatest victories in history. At Antietam he attacked what he thought was a partial enemy army, stunned it with heavy blows, and then at the decisive moment held out his reserve. Lee retired to Virginia and McClellan proclaimed to the government that he had won a "complete victory." Not unreasonably Lincoln thought this meant that he had smashed up the Confederates and was now about to destroy them. All that McClellan meant was that the enemy had left his front. It was his last demonstration of make-believe. Lincoln relieved him from command and he would never return.

To the last, McClellan could never see that he was responsible in any way for the failure of any of his military operations. His convicton that he had made no errors was not unnatural, was, in fact, the same assurance most unsuccessful generals comforted themselves with when they looked back at their careers. What was uncommon and

"Grasp of
reality
frail?"

unnatural in McClellan's analysis was his ascription of the cause of his downfall—the government had deliberately and almost from the start set out to destroy him. That McClellan could believe such a thing is indicative of his overdeveloped ego and his sense of persecution. But more, it reveals him as a man whose grasp of reality was so frail as to approach neuroticism. McClellan actually thought that in dealing with the government he could define the terms of his co-operation and the limits of his responsibility. He assumed, as somebody has said, that George B. McClellan and the government were equal contracting parties.

Again a series of quotations from his private letters will illustrate a facet of his character. In the Virginia campaign, as he fancied the enemy army was outgrowing his: "My government, alas, is not giving me any aid. . . . The Government has deliberately placed me in this position. If I win, the greater the glory. If I lose, they will be damned forever, both by God and men." To Secretary of War Stanton, on the eve of the Seven Days: "I regret my great inferiority, in numbers, but feel that I am in no way responsible for it. . . . But if the result of the action . . . is a disaster, the responsibility cannot be thrown on my shoulders;

it must rest where it belongs." To Stanton, at the end of the Seven Days: "I have lost this battle because my force was too small. . . . I am not responsible for this. . . . I have seen too many dead and wounded comrades to feel otherwise than that the government has not sustained this army. . . . If I save this army now, I tell you plainly that I owe no thanks to you or to any other persons in Washington. You have done your best to sacrifice this army." On his growing doubts that he or his army should continue to serve the tricksters of politics: "I have lost all regard and respect for the majority of the administration, & doubt the propriety of my brave men's blood being spilled to further the designs of such a set of heartless villains. . . . They are aware that I have seen through their villainous schemes, & that if I succeed my foot will be upon their necks." When he was restored to active command after Second Bull Run: "Again I have been called upon to save the country. . . . I felt that under the circumstances no one else *could* save the country." After Antietam and after he had demanded of Lincoln that as a condition of his continued service Secretary Stanton and General in Chief Halleck be removed: "The only safety for the country and me is to get rid of both of them. . . . I feel it is now time for the country to come to my help and remove these difficulties from my path. . . . I feel that I have done all that can be asked in twice saving the country. If I continue in its service I have at least the right to demand a guarantee that I shall not be interfered with."

No general can afford, for his own or his country's good, to deny all responsibility for all his actions, to throw off on his government the responsibility for defeat, to prescribe to his government the conditions on which he will serve. In a democracy not even a general who wins great victories can do these things. McClellan did all of them and never won a great victory, and inevitably he fell. He failed because of the kind of man he was, and the man made the kind of general he was. The judgment of Kenneth P. Williams may be altered to secure a final verdict.

McClellan was a real general, but he never grasped reality. McClellan was a truthful soldier, but he could not see things in their true light. McClellan was an attractive but deluded man, with considerable military knowledge and little knowledge of his country, who sat a horse well and wanted life to be as he thought it should be.

42

William Tecumseh Sherman

---◆◆---

SHERMAN'S LIFE UP TO 1861 was a record of small successes, large failures, and frustrated ambitions. In the first year of the war and in his first important command he underwent a mental collapse and endured the humiliation of being called insane in the public press. Transferred to a lesser position in the Western theater, he demonstrated sound qualities as a subordinate officer, and coming under the command and the influence of U. S. Grant his star rose with Grant's. He came to command a corps in Grant's army and to be his superior's favorite and most favored assistant. William Tecumseh Sherman owed a great debt to Grant and he expressed it without reserve and in many forms. Once he said with a lightness that pointed up his feelings the more: "General Grant is a great general. I know him well. He stood by me when I was crazy and I stood by him when he was drunk; and now, sir, we stand by each other always."

When Grant went east in 1864 to assume the direction of all the Union armies, Sherman took over as the commander of the largest field army in the West. Now his own fame would be born. He led his free-swinging and freebooting host through the heart of the Confederacy in one of the great marches of military history. He brought a new and a terrible kind of war to America and to the world. His men, who viewed him with a peculiarly possessive affection, vowed they would follow such a general as "Uncle Billy" to the ends of the earth, and the newspapers, which had once called him crazy, now hailed him in such extravagant terms as "Tecumseh the Great." At the end of the war he stood second only to Grant in the North's hall of heroes, and there were some who thought he should stand first. And there were some too who thought he deserved no standing at all.

Sherman's contemporaries were not alone in dividing over his reputation. The question of where to rank him as a soldier has troubled military analysts ever since the war. Probably no other general has been placed in so many and such dissimilar categories. He has been called the prophet of total war and the most modern-minded soldier of his war; a master strategist who employed strategy so brilliantly that tactics, that is, fighting, became subordinate or unnecessary; and a planner ahead of his time whose operations foreshadowed the panzer dashes and the strategic bombing of World War II.

He has also been classified as a mere raider on a gigantic scale; as a general who saw and persued only geographical objectives; and as a soldier who because of some mistrust of himself avoided the decision of battle. One critic, admitting that Sherman exhibited many of the traits of a great commander, points out that never once did he command in a battle where he engaged his whole force and that he never won a resounding victory. Sherman stands in history as perhaps the supreme paradox among the generals of either side, but like most paradoxical characters his apparent contradictions can be resolved. Actually he was many of the things that were said about him. The answer to the Sherman enigma is to be found in his education and background, in the cast of his mind, in his early personal associations in the war, and in the philosophy of war which he came to cherish. And, as with McClellan, whom he was startlingly like, it is to be found in his temperament or personality. He represents a step of progression beyond McClellan's kind of generalship, but his was not the final step. Still another by another general would be required before the nation could marshal its resources for final victory.

Sherman is one of the most described generals of the war. He attracted attention from all observers and especially from the newspaper correspondents. He affected to detest the reporters and tried to bar them from his lines. They, in many cases, reciprocated his feeling but found him copy too good to ignore. One painted him thus: "When I first saw him in Missouri . . . his eye had a half-wild expression, probably the result of excessive smoking. . . . Sherman was never without a cigar. . . . He looks rather like an anxious man of business than an ideal soldier, suggesting the exchange and not the camp. Sometimes he works for twenty consecutive hours. He sleeps little; nor do the most powerful opiates re-

lieve his terrible cerebral excitement." Another
wrote that Sherman was "built narrow and almost
effeminate" and that his eyes flashed incessantly
in every direction when he walked, talked, or
laughed. This reporter added revealingly that
Sherman "walked, talked or laughed all over. He
perspired thought at every pore." A third noted
that Sherman was lean in features and build and
that his "quick movements denoted good muscle
added to absolute leanness, not thinness."

Army officers who came into contact with Sherman reacted exactly as the correspondents did.
One general depicted him at a camp meal, sitting
on a cracker box before a rough table and too
busy to eat: "He talked and smoked cigars incessantly, giving orders, dictating telegrams, bright
and chipper." An officer who called on him at Savannah was fascinated by the spectacle he saw:
"If I were to write a dozen pages I could not tell
you a tenth part of what he said, for he talked incessantly and more rapidly than any man I ever
saw. General Sherman is the most American man
I ever saw, tall and lank, with hair like thatch,
which he rubs up with his hands. . . . It would
be easier to say what he did not talk about than
what he did. . . . At his departure I felt it a re-

lief and experienced almost an exhaustion after the excitement of his vigorous presence." And a sensitive staff officer who saw Sherman when he visited Grant's lines at Petersburg thought that all his features expressed "determination, particularly the mouth, which is wide and straight with lips shut tightly together." Sherman was a "remarkable-looking man," this observer concluded, "such as could not be grown out of America—the concentrated quintessence of Yankeedom." The same impressions run through all these pen sketches—a nature of explosive nervous energy and almost manic elation; a mind playing restlessly on all manner of subjects, military and otherwise; an appearance not martial but like a man of business; and a type unique but peculiarly American. Together they tell us a great deal about Sherman the man and Sherman the general. Nobody would have thought of writing such things about George B. McClellan.

On the eve of the war Sherman was a man with a burning desire for distinction. To him life was a fierce competition and a challenge to excel. He once wrote, in the war, when he had made a name but knew his greatest fame was still before him: "Life is a race, the end is all that is remembered by the Great World. Those, who are out at the end, will never be able to magnify the importance of intermediate actions, no matter how brilliant and important."

It is possible that his earliest surroundings had something to do with his ambition. After his father's death, the numerous Sherman brood were placed around in the homes of friends and relatives. Young Sherman was raised in the home of Thomas Ewing, a wealthy and prominent Ohio political figure, whose daughter Ellen he eventually married. In part, Sherman's constant strivings may have been an unconscious attempt to show the prosperous Ewings what he could do. But before the war he failed to realize any of his goals. After graduating from West Point he had a respectable, although not an especially noteworthy, career in the army. He finally resigned his commission, obviously with the hope of making more money in civilian pursuits. He tried banking and failed, and he tried law and failed. In 1859 he accepted the superintendency of a military school in Louisiana and thought at last he had found a place where he could be satisfied. But hardly had he got the school in operation when the secession movement swept the Lower South and Louisiana joined the parade of states out of the Union. An ardent nationalist, Sherman felt that he had no recourse but to resign his position.

He went to St. Louis, where he engaged in the street railway business and watched with skeptical eyes the first frenzied efforts of the government to prepare for civil conflict. Unlike McClellan, he had known grim failure. But adversity had not strengthened his inner fiber any more than success had McClellan's. Nor had his civilian experience given him any firmer grasp of reality than McClellan possessed. He craved security and deference and was morbidly sensitive to disagreement or inattention. Particularly irritating to him was the apparent refusal of politicians and other people to take seriously his warnings that the South was in deadly earnest. He doubted that a mass democracy had the fortitude to sustain a prolonged war or that a government of politicians could effectively prosecute a major military effort.

Despite his seeming withdrawal from the scenes around him, Sherman was quite willing to accept a particular kind of position in the military organization. He spurned the offer of a major general of volunteers commission from Missouri and informed the War Department he preferred a

lower grade in the regular army. He finally took
the colonelcy of the 13th Regular Infantry Regiment. Ostensibly his reason for refusing a rank
other men would have jumped at was that volunteers were too undisciplined to be used as in-
vaders and that the job should be handled by
regulars. Unquestionably at this stage Sherman
was prejudiced against citizen soldiers and did
not want to be associated with them. It is also
possible that he was unconsciously seeking a subordinate place as a shelter from responsibility,
that from frustration he had developed a neu-
rosis that made him doubt himself. This analysis
takes on added plausibility in the light of events
that followed. After the battle of First Bull Run,
where he commanded a brigade, he was named
a brigadier general of volunteers and assigned as
second in command to Robert Anderson in Kentucky. Before he left Washington he apparently
extracted a promise from Lincoln or somebody in
high authority that under no condition would he
be asked to take over the direction of the department. But soon General Anderson's health failed,
and Sherman, as the number two man on the spot,
was shoved into the top command.

Now ensued an episode that eclipsed McClellan's wildest mental gymnastics. In a seeming

panic, Sherman telegraphed Lincoln: "I am ordered to command here. I must have a few experienced brigadiers. I will not be responsible for events but will do my best." He saw on every hand increasing dangers from increasing numbers of Confederates, and he demanded of the War Department heavier and heavier reinforcements. The situation got to the point where Secretary of War Cameron, returning to Washington from St. Louis, decided to stop off in Louisville to talk to the perturbed general personally. Unfortunately for all concerned and especially for Sherman, the interview took place in the presence of the party accompanying Cameron, which included several newspaper reporters. Sherman, striding up and down the room and talking and gesticulating in his customary excitable way, made a bad impression. Apparently he said that a minimum of 60,000 men would be required in the department for defensive purposes and 200,-000 for an offensive. Later there would be dispute as to how he meant to employ the 200,000. Cameron understood that this large a host would be needed to clear the Kentucky front, whereas Sherman insisted he had been talking about occupying the whole Mississippi Valley.

Regardless of the exact language used, Sher-

Ky — relieved & sent to St. Louis

man had asked for the impossible. At that time the government could no more have raised the 200,000 he wanted than it could have the 273,000 requested by McClellan. And he had asked in the worst possible way, with a display of nervous emotion and in the presence of his enemies the reporters. Soon stories began appearing in the press detailing the interview and implying broadly that he was insane. Humiliated and oppressed, he asked to be relieved. He was assigned to duty at St. Louis, but after a short stay there he asked for leave to go home to rest. After a period he came back to St. Louis, a subdued but apparently a more serene man.

Later in the war, when the government put into the Western theater total forces approximating those demanded by Sherman in 1861, it appeared that he had been right. People said that Sherman had not been insane after all but only farseeing or that if he was crazy he was crazy like a fox. It was a swing of opinion that Sherman and his friends did everything to foster, and the revised verdict has been accepted as correct by history. Actually the situation as it developed did not follow the pattern predicted by Sherman, nor did it completely sustain his position. The Federal forces in the vast Western theater operated, as they had to, in subtheaters, the two principal ones being the Mississippi River line and the Tennessee River line. And they operated generally as two field armies, neither of which was anything near the 200,000 mark recommended by Sherman. The largest Federal army in the West, the one which Sherman himself commanded in 1864, numbered at the most 100,000.

Sherman's original estimate of the situation was not the product of a cool and analytical mind but of a fevered and distraught imagination. By the testimony of the most unimpeachable witnesses Sherman suffered in 1861, to put it in the mildest terms, a mental collapse. When his wife heard that something was amiss, she hastened to Louisville and from there wrote his brother, Senator John Sherman: "Knowing insanity to be in the family and having seen Cump on the verge of it in California, I assure you I was tortured by fears, which have been only in part relieved since I got here." Her husband's mind had been wrought up to a "morbid state of anxiety," she continued, and was in an "unhealthy state." Later from their home where Sherman was resting she confided to John: "If there were no kind of insanity in your family and if his feelings were not already in a morbid state I would feel less concern about him, but as it is I cannot bear to have him go back to St. Louis haunted by the specter and reading the effects of it in any apparent insubordination of officers or men. It will induce and fasten upon him that melancholy insanity to which your family is subject." Sherman himself confessed to his brother that there was no excuse for his exhibition: "I am so sensible now of my disgrace from having exaggerated the force of our enemy in Kentucky that I do think I should have committed suicide were it not for my children. I do not think that I can again be entrusted with a command."

It would be some time before anybody would want to give him an independent command. At St. Louis, the departmental commander, General Henry W. Halleck, who knew Sherman from before the war, thought a useful place could be found for the depressed officer. He began to draw Sherman into conferences on strategy and showed in other ways that he still believed in him. Halleck demonstrated his confidence most strongly by assigning Sherman to command the Cairo district, formerly under Grant and a part of Grant's rear zone in the movement against Forts Henry and Donelson. Sherman co-operated loyally with Grant, forwarding troops to the front, and after the fall of the forts he joined Grant with a division of volunteers.

Now began the great partnership of Grant and Sherman, the association that would profoundly influence Sherman's whole personality and later career. As division and then corps commander he experienced with Grant the anguish of Shiloh, where as subordinate he showed up somewhat better than Grant did as superior; the boredom of Corinth, where he claimed to have persuaded Grant, despondent over a temporarily inactive role, not to leave the army; and the glory of Vicksburg, where he questioned the boldness of Grant's final move and then overflowed with admiration at his accomplishment.

Sherman blossomed under Grant's supervision. He became sure of himself. He was deft and decisive on the field and able and fertile in counsel. In some way the stolid and apparently prosaic Grant gave the mercurial and seemingly more brilliant Sherman a poise and a balance theretofore lacking. Sherman himself was aware of the transformation and of Grant's part in it, and he analyzed it with a realism that reflected his growing sense of security. In a revealing letter to Grant, Sherman said that his superior's strongest feature was a "simple faith in success." He went on to confess: "Also, when you have completed your best preparations you go into battle without hesitation . . . no doubts, no reserve; and I tell you that it was this that made me act with confidence. I knew wherever I was that you thought of me, and that if I got in a tight place you would come—if alive."

To a friend Sherman volunteered a more introspective explanation: "Wilson, I am a damn sight smarter than Grant. I know a great deal more about war, military history, strategy, and grand tactics than he does; I know more about organization, supply, and administration, and about everything else that he does. But I tell you where he beats me, and where he beats the world. He don't care a damn for what the enemy does out of his sight, but it scares me like hell. . . . I am more nervous than he is. I am more likely to change my orders, or to countermarch my command than he is. He uses such information as he has, according to his best judgment. He issues his orders and does his level best to carry them out without much reference to what is going on about him."

At first glance it might seem that in these remarks Sherman was saying only that he had too much imagination and that Grant had none. But in his typically explosive style Sherman was ascribing the highest quality of generalship to Grant —the character to dominate any situation and the inertia of war. Because Grant had character, Sherman told one officer, all others could easily subordinate themselves to him with absolute trust.

The question that Sherman ultimately would have to face was: Did he have this kind of character himself? He was clearly a fine subordinate, an outstanding corps commander. Grant considered him the best in his command and obviously had him marked for promotion. After the Federal debacle at Chickamauga in 1863 Grant was named commander of all armies in the West. He went to Chattanooga to inspect the beleaguered army there and decided to break the Confederate strangle hold by bringing in reinforcements for an offensive. His first thought was to call Sherman to him with part of Grant's own army. The movement succeeded, although Sherman's part in it was not too glorious.

Then in 1864 Grant was called to Washington to take over the supreme command of all Union armies. He decided to combine the forces at Chattanooga into something resembling a modern army group under Sherman's command. The mission of this aggregation was to strike for Atlanta and to destroy the Confederate army in Georgia. Thus Sherman was to lead one of the major offensives that were calculated to break the back of the Confederacy.

Now Sherman would be on his own, without the reassuring presence of Grant. All of his field experience had been as a subordinate. Only twice had he exercised independent command: in Kentucky, where he had collapsed under the strain, and in Mississippi early in 1864, where he conducted a marauding expedition that met no opposition. Many questions might be asked about this unusual man with his unusual background as he stood on the verge of his first great test. How would he bear up under the lonely responsibility of independent command? Other generals in the war were jumped up from corps to army command, but none of them had Sherman's peculiar psychology or had come to rely on an image as he had on Grant. How would he react when he and not Grant had to determine what the enemy was doing out of sight? What kind of general was he anyway? Was he, in fact, a general at all, in the sense of being a battle captain who could rise above the inertia of war? And if he was not a battle captain, what was he?

Sherman was many things and many men. He had too many facets to be a great fighting soldier. Perhaps he recognized this flaw in himself when he said that Grant's strongest feature was a simple faith in success. Sherman's brilliant mind and spreading imagination played over too wide an area to focus on any single goal. He was, although he would have indignantly denied it, a journalist. His reports and official letters sparkle with expressions designed to attract reader attention, and his postwar memoirs are far above the average reminiscent account in interest and literary style. In truth, Sherman's bitter feuds with the reporters may be set down as a difference between technicians. Each party recognized the other for what he was.

He was a political philosopher, and this may explain his diatribes against politicians. Like McClellan, he knew very little about the working of the American democratic system or the nature of democratic politicians. What he did know made him contemptuous of both. He thought that politicians, including the civilian directors of the government, should keep their hands completely off the military machine and the conduct of the war.

Like some other soldiers in our history who have had the same concept of the soldier as a

Sherman not a democrat or for blacks

free agent (McClellan is an example in the Civil War), Sherman continually pronounced on political issues and intruded his views on the political sphere. He had very definite convictions as to what the policy objectives of the government should be and what they should not be. Most notably, the war must not turn into a crusade to free the slaves or alter significantly the pattern of race relations. Sherman had the most rigid opinions on the race question. The colored race was inferior, he believed, and must be kept in a subordinate position. "Iron is iron and steel is steel," he once announced, "and all the popular clamor on earth will not impart to one the qualities of the other. So a nigger is not a white man, and all the Psalm singing on earth won't make him so." He opposed the employment of Negroes as soldiers on the ground that those who held the sword at the war's end would hold the power and that the power must be restricted to the white race.

Sherman's motives in supporting the war and in prosecuting it as terribly as he eventually would are difficult to untangle. Obviously he was not moved by any devotion to extend a democratic principle or any desire to elevate a submerged race. As much as anything, Sherman acted out of a passion for the maintenance of authority, sym-

bolized in this case by the American nation, and
out of an outraged conviction that the South had
without cause flouted a legal authority. On
several occasions he openly proclaimed a pref-
erence for monarchy over democracy, suggesting
that the "self-interest of one man" could be a
"safer criterion than the wild opinions of ignorant
men." The American government might not be
perfect, but it still represented authority and
had to be obeyed. As he saw it, the issue was
that simple: "All I pretend to say, on earth as in
heaven, man must submit to an arbiter. He must
not throw off his allegiance to his Government or
his God without just reason and cause. The South
had no cause—not even a pretext. . . . Had we
declined battle, America would have sunk . . .
meriting the contempt of all mankind."

He was finally, and perhaps most significantly,
an early student of what would later be called
geopolitics: the relation between the physical en-
vironment of a people and their domestic and foreign policies. At some time before the war Sherman had developed a mystic concept of the
Mississippi River and Valley as a heartland bind-
ing together the Union in an indivisible whole. It
was this great center that made America unique
and great and worth preserving. He told one

Southerner on the eve of hostilities: "Were it not for the physical geography of the country it might be that people would consent to divide and separate in peace. But the Mississippi is too grand an element to be divided and all its extent must of necessity be under one government."

Once the war started all his thinking focused on measures to regain control of the national river. As he frankly confessed, his determination on this question went beyond normal bounds: "To secure the safety of the Mississippi River I would slay millions. On that point I am not only insane but mad." The correspondence between him and Grant after the fall of Vicksburg offers a perfect contrast between the minds of the two men. Grant regarded the opening of the river in a strictly military light and began to think about the next move. Sherman viewed it as a great political event and wanted to contemplate the results. On the day Vicksburg surrendered he wrote to Grant: "I did want rest, but I ask nothing until the Mississippi River is ours, and Sunday and 4th of July are nothing to Americans till the river of our greatness is free as God made it." In a congratulatory address to his troops he said that it would be a matter of pride to them and their children that they had a part in making the river again free, thus assuring the future greatness of their country: "Let the magnificent result give to all new hope and assurance that, by discipline, by patient industry, by courage and confidence in our country and cause, the United States of America will instead of sinking into Mexican anarchy, arise with proud honor and glory, and become what Washington designed it—'The freest and best regulated Government on earth.'"

In Sherman's strategic thinking the heartland took precedence over all other theaters. Here the issue of the war would be decided and here the great generals of the war would emerge and should remain. "The man who at the end of this war holds the military control of the Valley of the Mississippi," he predicted, "will be *the* man." He begged Grant not to act as supreme commander from the East but to establish his headquarters in the West: "For God's sake and your country's sake, come out of Washington! . . . Come West; take to yourself the whole Mississippi Valley. Let us make it dead-sure, and I tell you the Atlantic slope and Pacific shores will follow its destiny as sure as the limbs of a tree live or die with the main trunk. . . . Here lies the seat of the coming empire; and from the West when our task is done, we will make short work of Charleston and Richmond and the impoverished coast of the Atlantic."

This man who would lead his army against Atlanta in 1864, was, then, an imaginative thinker and a political scientist and a social philosopher as well as a soldier. For him war and victory were not ends in themselves but means to greater ends. There still remained this doubt about him: Was he enough of a soldier to employ the force required to achieve victory? In preparing his campaign and in executing it he would demonstrate another aspect of his varied talents. He would prove to be a great engineer and a master of logistics. He moved to Atlanta along a railroad line of communications, and to ensure that this line would always be safe he worked out elaborate precautionary arrangements. A movable railroad base with repair utensils and crews trained in rebuilding lines and bridges destroyed by enemy raiding parties made it possible for the army to advance with no serious supply difficulties. Sherman's troops were so adept at mending damaged facilities that the legend arose in the Confederate ranks that the general carried duplicate tunnels and bridges along with him.

But Sherman knew that he could not be bound too tightly to the railroad, that in penetrating the reaches of Georgia he would have to possess the freedom to strike out on occasion from the line of track. So he organized a system of horse and wagon transportation that would provide adequate sustenance without sacrificing mobility. Neglecting no detail, he studied the United States census reports for Georgia and the tax rolls of Georgia counties, and thus learned the areas most able to furnish food for his men and animals. In the Georgia campaign he introduced engineering as a major factor in modern warfare. He introduced other modern devices as well: map coordinates, the photographic duplication of maps, trip wires, and a looser and more extended order of infantry attack.

In the end he won Atlanta. In a campaign of seventeen weeks he moved the military front over a hundred miles southward. The economic and human resources of Atlanta and north Georgia were now lost to the South. He accomplished all of his mission except the most important part. He failed to destroy the Confederate army, which remained intact and was still a force to be reckoned with. The advance to Atlanta is usually pictured as a campaign of maneuver, as a gigantic chess game in which Sherman and his wily opponent, Joseph E. Johnston, moved their pieces without ever coming to grips. The image is accurate in part but not completely so. In the whole campaign there was, with the possible exception of Kenesaw Mountain, no major or set battle. But there was constant skirmishing and small fighting. The casualty total for the Federal army was a respectable 38,000. Still the fact remains that Sherman did not succeed in bringing the enemy to a show-down battle.

It can be argued that he failed because of the skill of Johnston in avoiding a showdown or because Johnston was constitutionally averse to facing a decision. With equal logic, it can be contended that it was Sherman who avoided a decision. As some critics see it, although Sherman had freed himself from many of the dogmas of traditional warfare, he was still bound by tradition; and in the Atlanta campaign he was guilty of pursuing a geographical rather than a military objective, of judging the occupation of a place more important than the destruction of an enemy army. Other critics suspect that Sherman was simply not a battle captain, that alone he lacked the confidence to handle troops in battle, that without Grant he would not risk greatly to win finally. There may be some truth in all these guesses. But it is more likely that at this stage

[handwritten margin note: fell into old strategy]

Sherman was not interested in either battle or territory as means to win a war. His brooding, imaginative mind had fixed on another strategy, and this he proceeded to employ after he seized Atlanta.

As Sherman approached Atlanta, the Confederate government had replaced Johnston the retreater with John B. Hood the fighter. Hood struck vigorously at the converging Federal columns but could not halt them. After standing a short siege he evacuated the city and retired southward. Sherman followed the Confederates for thirty miles and then returned to Atlanta. He has been severely criticized for relaxing his pressure and for not pushing the foe to the death. The curious result of his move was to restore the initiative to Hood, who was now free to move as he willed and who proceeded to hit the Federal line of rail communications running back to Chattanooga. Although Sherman acted to protect the railroad, he made no real move against Hood. His excuse was that he would never be able to bring Hood to battle or run him to earth and that he did not propose to flit all over Georgia and Alabama in an empty chase. There was merit in this, but it was essentially an excuse.

Sherman had no interest in seeking out Hood.

He had devised another plan of operations, breath-taking in its boldness, which he now broached to Grant. Simply, it was this: He would send back to Tennessee as a defensive force 30,000 troops under General Thomas. With the remaining 60,000 he would march across Georgia on a wide front, destroying economic resources as he moved, and come out at some point on the seacoast from which he could be transported by water to join Grant before Richmond. (The point turned out to be Savannah, and instead of continuing by sea he marched through the Carolinas.)

The plan was breath-taking also in its possible risks. Sherman assumed that Hood would not follow him—the operation would have been impossible with an opposing field army in his front—but would head for Tennessee. He further assumed that Thomas could gather enough strength to him to repel Hood, else Sherman would have to return to do the job himself. As it happened, everything developed as Sherman hoped it would. Hood went to Tennessee and was defeated at Nashville, and Sherman marched over Georgia virtually unimpeded. But it is quite possible that it might have been very different. Hood, if he had advanced quickly enough, before the defending forces were concentrated, might have caused enough trouble to bring Sherman back; and if that had happened, the whole Federal victory schedule would have been disrupted, with incalculable effects on the outcome of the war. For a general who risked rarely on the field Sherman risked too much in strategy.

The plan which Sherman now put into action had evolved slowly, but the germ of it had long been with him. It could have come only from a mind like his, a mind that nourished mystic concepts of authority and natural unity and was capable of indulging in the most violent excesses of thought and of translating these excesses into action. One commentator has suggested that at this stage Sherman seemed to be possessed by a kind of manic elation that was another side of his earlier depression. "I am satisfied, and have been all the time," he declared with cold excitement, "that the problem of this war consists in the awful fact that the present class of men who rule the South must be killed outright rather than in the conquest of territory."

Other Northern generals would grasp and employ the concept of war against civilians, but none would do it with Sherman's relish and detail or understand its implications as he did or place it on the same broad philosophical level. It is com-

72

monly and loosely said that Sherman inaugurated economic warfare against the Confederacy and introduced this practice of modern war to the world. The generalization does not do justice to either Sherman's purpose or his strategy. He did destroy immense amounts of property in Georgia and the Carolinas, but even marching, as he usually did, on a sixty-mile front, he could touch only a fraction of the total resources left to the Confederacy. His real objective, as he carefully explained, was the mind of the South. He would convince the Southern people that their cause was hopeless and that the promise of victory held out by President Jefferson Davis was completely empty, and he would do this with such an overwhelming display of strength that nobody could misread the message.

He outlined the effects to Grant: "I propose to act in such a manner against the material resources of the South as utterly to negative Davis' boasted threat and promises of protection. If we can march a well-appointed army right through his territory, it is a demonstration to the world, foreign and domestic, that we have a power which Davis cannot resist. This may not be war but rather statesmanship, nevertheless it is overwhelming to my mind that there are thousands of people abroad and in the South who reason thus: 'If the North can march an army right through the South, it is proof positive that the North can prevail.'" He put it in similar fashion to another officer: "I attach more importance to these deep incisions into the enemy's country, because this war differs from European wars in this particular: we are not only fighting armies, but a hostile people, and must make old and young, rich and poor, feel the hard hand of war, as well as their organized armies." And after the great march had ended he thus summarized its impact: "My aim then was to whip the Rebels, to humble their pride, to follow them to their inmost recesses, and to make them fear and dread us."

This, then, was economic warfare conducted for a psychological end, war against the popular will of the enemy, war against the enemy state sheltered behind its armies. It was startlingly modern and starkly effective. Sherman drove through Georgia and was at Savannah by December, 1864, and from there he crunched through South Carolina and was in North Carolina when the war ended. He had consummated one of the great engineering feats and one of the longest marches in the history of war. He had seriously sapped the economic strength of the

Confederacy, destroying or wrecking arsenals, factories, food supplies, and railroads in three states. He had beyond a doubt undermined the Southern will to resist. The spectacle of a Federal army flowing relentlessly across the land had much of the effect on public opinion that Sherman had envisioned. Soldiers in the Confederate army at Richmond deserted in droves to go home to protect their families in the line of Sherman's advance. Jefferson Davis warned: "Sherman's campaign has produced bad effects on our people. Success against his future operations is needful to animate public confidence.

Sherman had achieved all these results without having to engage in much serious fighting. This is the accomplishment, his admirers claim, that is his great contribution to the art of war; this it is that entitles him to rank among the great soldiers. He substituted strategy for tactics and made battles unnecessary. He proved that it was possible to strike at the vitals of an enemy without having to meet and defeat the enemy's army. He anticipated the theory and practice of modern air power. He was a strategist ahead of his time. In the latest listings Sherman appears as the most modern soldier of the Civil War.

There is too much easy exaggeration in all these

ascriptions. But Sherman tempts extravagant evaluation. He seems so original and so modern that we tend to study him as an isolated figure and to forget the factors in the total military situation that made it possible for him to do what he did. He could not have moved from Atlanta to the sea if Thomas had not held and defeated Hood at Nashville. He could not have moved from the sea to the Carolinas if Grant had not kept Lee's army pinned at Richmond. He advanced without fighting, but this was due not so much to his superior strategy as to the smallness of the army opposing him and to his unconcern for destroying it. The Confederate forces actually increased in numbers as he advanced and at the battle of Bentonville were strong enough to give him a bad scare.

It is dangerous and can result in a false perspective to push too far a parallel between Sherman and later ways and weapons. It is true that he performed with an army something resembling the function of a modern bomber force, but his army was not a force on wings and did not have the immunity of one. If he had been checked or defeated, the result could have been tragic for him and his cause.

We come finally with Sherman, as we did with McClellan and as we have to do with every sol-

Will of a nation with people.

dier, to the question that has to be answered. What kind of general was he? The answer must be that Sherman was one of the great soldiers of the Civil War. He moved the art of warfare significantly forward. More than any other general of his time, he understood that the will of a nation to fight rests on the economic and psychological security of its people and that if these supporting elements are destroyed all resistance may collapse. But his strategy alone would not have won the war. He hurt and weakened the Confederacy, but he could not bring it down. It would not fall until its principal army was brought to bay and defeated, and Sherman was not the man to deliver the last great blow. That would have to come from another general, one who made his best preparations and then went in without reserve or hesitation and with a simple faith in success.

Ulysses Simpson Grant

---◆---

GRANT'S LIFE IS, in some ways, the most remarkable one in American history. There is no other quite like it. His career before the war was a flat and a complete failure. He graduated from West Point with no distinction, standing almost exactly in the middle of his class. His service in the regular army was without any special note, and the experience was not altogether happy for him. He left the army, if not under a cloud, certainly with mutual relief to both parties. He essayed various business ventures, all of which ended in little or no success. On the eve of the war he was working in his father's leather goods store in Galena, Illinois, at a job he detested, an even more bitter and thwarted man than Sherman. During the war he rose successively from smaller unit commands to field army and departmental command and finally to supreme command of all Union armies. He directed the movements of over half a million troops on distant fronts, the largest force yet to be controlled by a single mind in the record of America's wars. After the war he was twice elected President and served in the highest office during one of the most difficult periods in our history. In the remaining years of his life he was regarded as a kind of unofficial first citizen, and even when he encountered business reverses in somewhat dubious associations he held the respect of his countrymen.

It is a life that began with failure and frustration and ended in success and glory, and it would seem that the man who acted it out should be accorded a fair measure of renown. And yet, oddly, the common verdict, which is also the verdict of history, is that Ulysses Simpson Grant was a failure in everything—in the army and in business before the war, in politics and as President, and again in business after the war. Even as a general he has stood in low repute. He did not fail in war, but he did not succeed because of any quality of greatness in himself. In the popular impression he was a hammerer and a butcher who was often drunk, an unimaginative and ungifted clod who eventually triumphed because he had such overwhelming superiority in numbers that he could hardly avoid winning. Once after the war he said wistfully that he had been ridiculed right up to Appomattox, and then suddenly they could not praise him enough. He has not come as yet, although there are signs a re-evaluation is under way, to his Appomattox in the literature of generalship.

People were always looking for visible signs of greatness in Grant. Most of them saw none and were disappointed. In appearance he was one of the most unimpressive of Civil War generals. He was five feet eight inches in height and carried his 135 pounds on a spare and slightly stooped frame. His chestnut-brown hair he wore short, and his full beard he kept close cut. The features were firm but not distinguished. Only the gray eyes, one of which was a little lower than the other, manifested much expression. He was given to long silences, and his speech, when it came, was slow and apparently embarrassed. Only when aroused did he speak at length or with feeling. His attire was always highly informal, and he conveyed in both dress and manner an aura of carelessness. Many who saw him remarked that he did not look like a soldier; they compared him, as some did Sherman but as none ever did Mc-Clellan, to somebody in a civilian occupation—a businessman, a country storekeeper, or a farmer.

It took the most sensitive of observers to penetrate past Grant's exterior to the real man. Colonel Theodore Lyman was such an individual, and when he first saw Grant in 1864 he was impressed. "His face has three expressions," Lyman noted, "deep thought; extreme determination; and great simplicity and calmness." The suggestion of iron determination fascinated Lyman, who again wrote: "He habitually wears an expression as if he had determined to drive his head through a brick wall, and was about to do it."

Another officer who also first glimpsed Grant in 1864 penned a more subtle analysis. Charles Francis Adams, Jr., grasped immediately the essence of Grant—that here was an extraordinary man who looked ordinary. Grant could pass for a "dumpy and slouchy little subaltern," Adams thought, but nobody could watch him without concluding that he was a "remarkable man. He handles those around him so quietly and well, he so evidently has the faculty of disposing of work and managing men, he is cool and quiet, almost stolid and as if stupid, in danger, and in a crisis he is one against whom all around, whether few in number or a great army as here, would instinctively lean. He is a man of the most exquisite judgment and tact."

Grant had none of the charismatic qualities that stirred troops to demonstrations at his appearance. He did not arouse the extravagant enthusiasm lavished on McClellan or the almost familial affection accorded to Sherman. In curious fact, the greatest of the Northern generals received the least popular attention of any officer in the war. Only once is it recorded that the men cheered him—when after the bloody meeting in the Wilderness he turned south. The soldiers had thought that like previous generals checked by Lee he would retire, and in their exhilaration at the unexpected advance they shouted as they marched past Grant sitting on his horse by the side of the road. But here the expression was more for the movement than for the man. Nearly always it was different. Even when he was at the height of his fame, and when his men were flushed with victory, he could ride along the lines without a sound being raised. But he never passed unnoticed. The soldiers would look up and utter such remarks as "There goes the old man," "Ulyss don't scare," or "Pretty hard nut for Johnny Reb to crack." This was the universal reaction of officers and men—a recognition voiced tersely or not at all that Grant was present and that things would be all right.

Once in the Vicksburg campaign he was directing the crossing of the army on a pontoon bridge over a bayou. He sat in the saddle calmly giving orders, and the men turned to note that this was their commander but said nothing. An officer who witnessed the scene pointed up a vital difference between Grant and another military type: "Here was no McClellan, begging the boys to allow him to light his cigar by theirs, or inquiring to what regiment that exceedingly fine marching company belonged. . . . There was no nonsense, no sentiment; only a plain businessman of the public, there for the one single purpose of getting that command over the river in the shortest time possible."

There was a difference between Grant and McClellan, or the types they represented, and, as the army came to realize surprisingly soon, the difference was in Grant's favor. One officer experienced a strange sensation at his introduction to Grant's generalship. He surveyed the field and found a new element present, and he recorded with a sense of wonderment: "I thought I detected in the management what I had never discovered before on the battlefield—a little common sense. Dash is handsome, genius glorious; but modest, old-fashioned, practical everyday sense is the trump, after all." People conditioned to the McClellan image of a general—as somebody in gorgeous apparel who pranced up on a horse and said something dramatic—found it hard to adjust to Grant and his ways.

But the army accomplished the transition with ease. To the soldiers there was nothing strange in the spectacle of Grant during the big assault at Vicksburg slouching in his saddle and whittling on a piece of wood and saying when the attack failed, "We'll have to dig our way in," in the tone, reported one correspondent, of a man saying it was bedtime. This was just "the old man" in perfect character. He had tried one move that had not turned out, and now he would try another. Wherever he was, he would try something; things would happen. The truest measurement of soldier opinion of Grant came from a sergeant. When this man heard Grant was in Sheridan's camp, he said pensively: "I hate to see that old cuss around.

When that old cuss is around there's sure to be a big fight on hand." The sergeant had also paid, perhaps, unwittingly, the supreme compliment to Grant's generalship.

Grant's initial service in the war was more fortunate in every way than the introductory experience of McClellan and Sherman. Unlike them, he was not pushed into high command before he was ready for it or before he had been tested for it. His first command was of a regiment, and then he was given a district, with headquarters at Cairo, Illinois. His superiors, first John C. Frémont and later Henry W. Halleck, did not trouble themselves too much about Grant, stuck off on the eastern rim of the Western Department; and he was free to proceed pretty much on his own, to test himself in situations of his own creating. Thus in November of 1861 he got up a small battle at a place called Belmont. The engagement was pointless and the result was in doubt, although the Confederates held the field at the end, but Grant had tried both himself and his men under fire. He had also learned a military lesson of inestimable value, which he may have known already and instinctively—that in war the side that attacks holds the initiative.

Most important for Grant's future development

was the opportunity he had in this early period to master the problems of command from the bottom up, to absorb the results of one situation before he moved on to another. At Cairo he was not exactly a small unit commander—he had 20,000 men under him—but his force was small enough for him to oversee it in detail. He had to deal with such prosaic matters as transportation facilities, ammunition supplies, rations, and maps, and he came to understand that these were the apparently little things that made up the spirit of an army. He came to know too that a commander had to be an administrator as well as a fighter, and he learned this lesson in far easier circumstances than did McClellan struggling to direct his massive host in the East. Always Grant learned something, from people around him and from the events of which he was a part. The most salient feature of the Grant war story is that it is a record of steady progression.

Early in 1862 Grant won Halleck's permission to attack Forts Henry and Donelson holding the center of the Confederate line in Kentucky. He captured both, the first easily and the second after a sharp fight, and suddenly he found that he was a national hero. He had achieved the first important Northern victory of the war; and his terms to the Confederates at Donelson, "Unconditional Surrender," according perfectly with his initials and composed, although unconsciously, with the skill of a public relations artist, caught the imagination of the whole country.

At Donelson Grant learned something he never forgot. Here the issue hung for a critical moment in the balance. Grant ordered an attack and carried the day. The lesson was that in every battle there came a time when both sides paused in exhaustion and that was when the outcome was decided—the general who had the moral courage to continue fighting would win.

After the fall of the forts Grant prepared to follow the retiring Confederates south. Although restricted by Halleck's cautious instructions, he had the instinct to push the enemy as hard as possible. He moved his army up (southward) the Tennessee River. Then ensued an episode that taught Grant another lesson. The episode concerned human relations, and the lesson was a hard one.

From the beginning of the war Grant moved under a cloud of suspicion and prejudice. It dated from his army days and involved the charge of drunkenness. Many in the army and some out of it supposed him to be a habitual inebriate. Regardless of the facts, the damning reputation clung to Grant. If he slipped while walking, if he was thrown from a horse, if he was sick, the cry went up that he was drunk again. It always went up if something went amiss in any of his battles. People constantly warned Lincoln that he was sustaining a drunken general. One prominent editor wrote the President that Grant was "a jackass in the original package. He is a poor drunken imbecile. He is a poor stick sober." An irresponsible officer went to the length of preferring, without trustworthy evidence, official charges against Grant. The specifications were so extreme as to be absurd: Drinking with traitors and vomiting all over the floor, "conduct unbecoming a gentleman and an officer"; and drinking with a harlot and having to crawl upstairs on all fours, "conduct not becoming a man." The truth seems to be that he drank when unhappy or lonely and that he was quickly affected by a few drinks. There is no evidence that he was under the influence at any moment of decision or that the habit interfered with his generalship. But the suspicion was always there, and it cropped up at regular intervals.

It cropped up notably after Grant started his Tennessee River advance. General Halleck was

unable to get any reports out of Grant—it turned
out this was the fault of a defecting telegraph op-
erator—and he jumped to the conclusion that
Grant had gone back to his old habit. After
some fluttery consultation with McClellan, then
general in chief, Halleck suspended Grant from
command. Eventually the misunderstanding
about the reports was cleared up, and Grant got
his army back. But Halleck continued to nourish
a mistrust of his subordinate who won battles.

Halleck, "Old Brains," the military scholar, was
the most traditional of soldiers and the most ex-
acting of martinets. He could not understand
Grant and he could not believe that Grant was a
good general. True, Grant managed somehow to
produce victories, but he did not conduct himself
properly between victories. Halleck rendered his
considered opinion on Grant's generalship in a
letter to the War Department. Written when
Grant had won the only substantial Northern tri-
umphs of the war, it was a remarkable document,
a damning self-indictment of the torpid type of
Northern leadership prevailing in the first phase
of the war. He had found Grant's army to be without discipline or order, Halleck reported, and the
fault lay with its commander: "I never saw a man
more deficient in . . . organization. Brave & able

on the field, he has no idea of how to regulate &
organize his forces before a battle or to conduct
the operation of a campaign."

Halleck was not the only person in authority to
be disturbed by Grant's neglect of punctilio.
Charles A. Dana, an observer for the War Department, on visiting Grant's headquarters was
shocked at the apparent laxity of the staff. Curiously, what bothered Dana most was that nobody, from Grant on down, could write or seemed
to be interested in writing! Illiteracy was the
pervading style, Dana snorted. From the cov-
ert sniping of Halleck and the overt snubs of others like him, Grant took another lesson. He
learned the virtues of patience and subordina-
tion.

After he resumed command of the Tennessee
River expedition, Grant disembarked his army at
a place called Pittsburg Landing. Nearby was a
country church called Shiloh, and here on two
April days in 1862 Grant would fight a battle he
had not expected to fight and would mark up still
one more addition to his education. At this point
Grant was flushed with confidence. He had ejected
the Confederates from Henry and Donelson and
had chased them along the Tennessee, and now,
if Halleck would let him, he would go after them

in their stronghold at Corinth, some twenty-five miles distant. He had convinced himself that the Confederate army in the West was on its last legs and that one more big battle would do it in. So at Pittsburg Landing he waited hopefully for word from Halleck to deliver the finishing blow. His camps were unfortified and open to attack. But then there would be no attack, because the Confederates were going to wait obligingly until the Federals were ready to move.

Grant was committing one of the most serious and most common errors in war—he was assuming that the enemy would do what he wanted them to do. And, like many other generals in history who made the same miscalculation, Grant was about to be confounded. The Confederates had no intention of co-operating with Grant. Rather, they were concentrating their forces for a destructive surprise attack at Shiloh, and the signs of what was coming were abundant and ominous, evident to everybody except Grant and his generals. On the day before the attack fell Grant said to one officer: "There will be no fight at Pittsburg Landing; we will have to go to Corinth, where the Rebels are fortified."

Regardless of all his denials later, Grant was surprised at Shiloh. More, he was brought close to a bad defeat that might have ended his career right there. But he managed to pull it out. He and his troops finally stemmed the Confederate rush on the first day, and on the second, with the aid of reinforcements from Don Carlos Buell, he pushed the foe from the field. Grant showed real character at Shiloh. Refusing to panic, he retained possession of himself and control over his army. He saved his army because he was able to dominate a bad situation. Later Grant did not like to talk about Shiloh. It was something he wanted to put behind him. But the experience of the battle was not forgotten. Never again would he underestimate the purpose of the enemy or neglect the vital principle of precaution.

Grant went into a period of eclipse after Shiloh. There was widespread criticism of his conduct of the battle and open imputations that he had been surprised because he was drunk. Halleck arrived at Pittsburg Landing to take command of the armies of Grant and Buell and to direct the advance on Corinth. Although Old Brains was not disposed to relieve Grant, he was convinced that his most vigorous general was too careless to be trusted. He relegated Grant to the harmless and frustrating position of second-in-command of the combined armies. Grant felt so useless that at one time, according to Sherman, he considered resigning his commission. But he hung on, and after the occupation of Corinth his fortunes took an upward turn again. The series of Union victories in the West, which Grant had set in motion at Henry and Donelson, had been won in Halleck's department, and although Grant was mainly responsible for the result, Halleck got the credit.

Old Brains seemed to be the most successful Northern field general, as well as a good administrator and a learned strategist, and in July, 1862, he was called to Washington to become general in chief of all Union armies. Before he left he split the Western Department into two commands under Buell and Grant. Characteristically, he assigned to Buell, who had done practically no fighting, a fighting mission—the seizure of well-guarded Chattanooga. To Grant, who had done much hard and victorious fighting, he gave the relatively inactive mission of protecting communications along the Mississippi River.

But at least Grant was in independent command again and free to plan the aggressive moves that were instinctive with him. He soon found his opportunity. In the winter of 1862 he advanced on Vicksburg, the fortress city that was the key to the whole Mississippi River line, beginning a campaign that continued until a July day in 1863.

Vicksburg is one of the classic campaigns of the Civil War and, indeed, of military history. It began with a traditional two-pronged advance from a base at Memphis. This movement failed, but instead of returning to Memphis and beginning a new attack, as the rules dictated, Grant shifted all his forces to the Mississippi. It turned into an apparent stalemate, with the Federals vainly seeking to approach Vicksburg over the marshy terrain north of the city. In the spring Grant unmasked his real plan, which he had matured in the winter months. Moving his army down the west side of the river while the navy ran by the enemy batteries, he crossed below the city and stood on dry ground. He faced two separate Confederate forces, one at Vicksburg and one at Jackson, which if united would outnumber him. Then the general called dull and unimaginative and a mere hammerer executed one of the fastest and boldest moves in the records of war. He struck the force at his rear and dissipated its threat and closed the one to his front in its fortress. In eighteen days he marched 200 miles, won four battles, and inflicted losses of 8,000 men and 88 guns on the foe.

After this brilliant demonstration the campaign settled into a siege. Tenacity took over from audacity and finally triumphed. Vicksburg fell and Grant rose to the apex of his career. Now there was none to carp. All hailed him as great. He became departmental commander of the whole Western theater, and in 1864 supreme commander over every theater.

Unknown to Grant, there was one who had marked him as great before Vicksburg and this individual's opinion was of some importance. As early as Henry and Donelson, Abraham Lincoln had noted that this Western general possessed some pleasingly rare qualities. Lincoln saw to it that Grant was promoted and followed closely the general's continued development. The reason for Lincoln's interest soon became evident. To a suggestion in the aftermath of Shiloh that Grant should be removed, the President replied simply: "I can't spare this man; he fights." Lincoln again sustained Grant during the Vicksburg siege. Some parties contended that Grant was wasting lives in a hopeless operation and should be relieved. Shrugging off the complaints, Lincoln said: "I

rather like the man. I think I'll try him a little longer." Lincoln liked Grant for several reasons. Not only would Grant fight, but he fought with the men and the tools he had at hand.

Every general in the war exaggerated the size of the enemy forces and tried to augment his own, and Grant was no exception. But he made his requests quietly, and if he was told that reinforcements were not available he made out with what he had. In this respect he was practically unique among Northern generals. Here was no Sherman collapsing at the specter of hosts gathering to destroy him or no McClellan always calling shrilly for more men and putting the responsibility for defeat on the government if he did not get them. A typical Grant application to Lincoln ran: "The greater number of men we have, the shorter and less sanguinary will be the war. I give this entirely as my views and not in any spirit of dictation—always holding myself in readiness to use the material given me to the best advantage I know how."

Lincoln was impressed by such restraint. He knew too many generals who wrote much and fought little. Once he remarked gratefully: "General Grant is a copious worker and fighter, but a very meager writer or telegrapher." The Presi-

dent expressed his fullest appreciation of Grant's reticence to a friend just before Vicksburg fell. "He doesn't worry and bother me," Lincoln said. "He isn't shrieking for reinforcements all the time. He takes what troops we can safely give him . . . and does the best he can with what he has got." Then Lincoln added: "And if Grant only does this thing right down there . . . why, Grant is my man and I am his the rest of the war."

Grant had done it right, and in 1864 he was the man, the central figure in the Union command system. He had demonstrated his capacities in every grade from regimental to departmental command, and now he was to face a greater test. In his position as supreme commander he would have to formulate strategy for the Union armies on many fronts and to oversee the execution of this strategy. And by his own choice he would direct, although not technically command, the field army that confronted the most dangerous Confederate army commanded by the man that most of the generals under him considered the greatest soldier of the war, Robert E. Lee.

In 1864 Grant stood in the full flower of his generalship. What manner of man was Lincoln's man and what kind of general was Lincoln's general? The man was a curious compound of many

things. Ourwardly solemn and shy, he could flash forth with bits of humor even in official documents. In the election of 1864 Lincoln through a friend requested permission to use a letter from Grant to prove there had been no presidential interference with army matters. Grant readily agreed to the President's quoting anything he had written but added: "I think, however, for him to attempt to answer all the charges the opposition will bring against him will be like setting a maiden to work to prove her chastity." Sometimes Grant's wit had a bite to it, as when he said a certain officer would "scarcely make a respectable Hospital nurse, if put in petticoats," or when he recommended that a general whom he disliked be stationed "at some convenient point on the northern frontier with the duty of detecting and exposing rebel conspiracies in Canada."

The man was—and in this he was much like Lincoln—a mixture of iron and velvet. He could send thousands of men into battle and to death without flinching. But he could be tremendously affected by the sight of wounded and especially maimed individuals. He could shatter Confederate armies with unrelenting and unending blows. But nobody was more capable of the knightly gesture to the defeated than this seemingly commonplace man. His conduct at Appomattox was not an inspiration of the moment or an isolated incident. He had manifested the same spirit in previous if lesser scenes.

One was recorded by a Confederate soldier who was taken prisoner at Chattanooga. As this man and other prisoners were being taken to the rear, they were halted to permit a group of Northern generals and their staffs to pass. The company jangled past the line of Confederates with no recognition except by one member. "When General Grant reached the line of ragged, filthy, bloody, starveling, despairing prisoners strung out on each side of the bridge, he lifted his hat and held it over his head until he passed the last man of that living funeral cortege. He was the only officer in that whole train who recognized us as being on the face of the earth."

Another Confederate prisoner recounted a similar example of Grant's consideration. This man was on a boat carrying exchanged Confederates back to Virginia; many of the men had been wounded before capture and had had amputations performed. While the boat was docked at Hampton Roads, Grant came aboard and had the men assembled. He made them an awkward yet moving little speech, telling them that the companies manufacturing artificial limbs were now turning out better products and assuring them that they would be able to lead useful lives.

Just as there were complexities in the man, so there were in the general. Grant was not by any means the simple soldier that he affected to be and that he has come to be in the myth. He was a general of parts. He had, first of all, a great store of common sense. And because he had this saving quality he was able to cope with all kinds of strange situations in this strange and modern war, situations that puzzled and even broke more traditional officers. Sherman, for example, could never adjust to the idea that the newspapers were going to report the war. He tried to drive the correspondents from his camp. Grant, on the other hand, accepted the reporters but controlled their activities so delicately that they were not sure what had happened to them. "General Grant informs us correspondents that he will willingly facilitate us in obtaining all information," one of them happily told his editor; he added, however, that the general was "not very communicative."

Because he had plain sense, Grant was capable of grasping the political nature of the war. This was the aspect of the conflict that McClellan raged at and Sherman sneered at. Grant took it for what it was, an inevitable and perhaps even a desirable concomitant of modern war. He understood, as did no other general on either side, that there was a relation between society and war, that sometimes in war generals had to act in response to popular or political considerations. The difference between him and Sherman on this score was dramatically illustrated in a discussion they had after the collapse of the first move against Vicksburg. Sherman argued that the army should return to Memphis and prepare for an entirely new campaign. This was the move prescribed in the books, but Grant replied that such a retrogression would discourage Northern opinion. Sherman said, as Grant quoted him, "that the politicians in Washington should take care of their affairs and we would take care of ours." This was the sentiment of the traditional soldier, but Grant the modern soldier saw the falsity of the dogma. "In a popular war," he recalled his answer to Sherman, "we had to consider political exigencies."

While Grant realized the connection between politics and war, he also knew it was not his job to propose policy to the government. Unlike McClellan and Sherman, who affected to despise

102

politicians but themselves were continually making political pronouncements, Grant avoided public and purple utterances. On the burning issue
of slavery and the war, he observed sensibly in
1861 that he would prefer to defeat the South
without interfering with its peculiar institution
but if slavery had to fall to save the nation it
should fall. "I have no hobby of my own with
regard to the Negro, either to effect his freedom
or to continue his bondage," he explained. "I do
not believe even in the discussion of the propriety
of laws and official orders by the army. One enemy at a time is enough." He held to this position
until the government made emancipation one of
the objectives of the war, and then he willingly
accepted the new policy. Informing Lincoln that
he would do all he could to further the project of
enlisting Negro soldiers, Grant said: "I would do
all this whether the arming of the Negro seemed
to me a wise policy or not, because it is an order
that I am bound to obey and I do not feel that
in my position I have a right to question any policy of the Government." He added characteristically that he would execute the policy with
relish because it would weaken the enemy.

One reason that Grant seems so simple in com-
parison with other generals is that he appears to

be unlearned and even unlettered in the art of war. Unlike McClellan and Sherman, he does not know history and doctrine; he has no brilliance; he employs only brute power; he bleeds his way to victory. This is the usual picture of Grant. But it is full of gaps. When he had to, Grant could be the most audacious of generals, as he proved in the Vicksburg campaign. His transfer in 1864 of the Army of the Potomac from northwestern Virginia through the Wilderness and across the James to Petersburg, all done without any diminishment of striking power, entitles him to be ranked with Sherman as an artist in logistics. He was, like practically every Civil War general, an indifferent tactician. He suffered heavy battle casualties but no more in proportion to his numbers engaged than any other commander. His total losses were among the highest in the war because he maintained a furious tempo of fighting.

It is true that Grant was not versed in doctrine, but his comparative ignorance was an advantage. Other generals were enslaved by their devotion to traditional methods. McClellan could not escape from the concept of war as bloodless maneuver directed at places. Sherman broke from the pattern to inaugurate a new way of war, but he never came to grips with the real resisting power of the Confederacy. Grant above all other Northern generals grasped the great truth that the ultimate objective in war is the destruction of the enemy's principal army. He once explained his theory of war. It was so apparently elementary that it was lost on most people then as it has been since: "The art of war is simple enough. Find out where your enemy is. Get at him as soon as you can. Strike at him as hard as you can and as often as you can, and keep moving on."

Actually, Grant knew more about doctrine than he cared to admit. He discussed its value often after the war. A knowledge of past battles could be helpful, he conceded, if the past did not become the master of the present. Too many Civil War generals tried to act as Napoleon or Frederick the Great had acted, but the rules of European wars could not be applied to the American scene. In one of his typical utterances, apparently simple but really extremely searching, Grant concluded: "War is progressive, because all the instruments and elements of war are progressive."

The theory of war expounded by Grant—seek out the enemy and strike him until he is destroyed —required the addition of a human factor. It could be executed only by a commander who possessed a tremendous will and a dominant personality. Grant had both. This, then, was his final and greatest quality—he had that indefinable force present in all the great battle captains that we call character.

Henry Adams saw this force in Grant and described it with characteristic condescension: "The type was pre-intellectual, archaic, and would have seemed so even to the cave-dwellers . . . men whose energies were the greater, the less they wasted on thought; men . . . more or less dull in outward appearance; always needing stimulants, but for whom action was the highest stimulant—the instinct of fight. Such men were forces of nature, energies of the prime."

An early English student of the war, C. F. Atkinson, expressed it more accurately and in the process explained why Grant seemed ordinary most of the time. Grant's character, said Atkinson, was under the command of a powerful will. But this will came into action only when stimulated by peculiar circumstances, which were battle and war. Then Grant acted, suddenly and violently. His action had its springs in his mind and was translated into deed by all the force of a paramount personality. When the stimulus passed, Grant lapsed into his usual pose. He seemed to be again what people took him for—a slouchy, commonplace little officer and man.

Grant would have need of all his strength of character in 1864. As supreme commander he framed a plan of grand strategy to attack the Confederacy on several fronts. He elected to accompany and direct the Federal army advancing on the most important front, the one held by Lee and his army. His instructions to Sherman and lesser commanders in other theaters were to make enemy armies their objective, and his directions to Meade, the titular head of the Eastern army, were the same: "Wherever Lee goes, there you will go also."

Grant traveled with Meade's army, in effect commanded it, for a definite purpose. Lee and Lee's army constituted the principal power of the Confederacy. Regardless of what happened in any other theater, the greatest power of the enemy had to be destroyed. Grant was determined to see to the job personally. He struck Lee in the savage and sustained battle of the Wilderness. It was the first meeting of the two greatest generals of the war, its only two who deserved to be ranked among the battle captains of history. Grant intended to force Lee to a showdown battle that would end the war immediately. He failed and recoiled with ghastly losses. The familiar pattern seemed about to repeat itself. A Federal general had attacked Lee and had been repelled, and now he would retire to lick his wounds, giving the Confederates time to regroup, and later, in weeks or months, he might come on again.

This was Grant's moment of crisis, and he met it. A reporter starting for Washington asked if the general had any message for the country. Grant thought a minute and said he had: "Well, if you see the President, tell him for me that, whatever happens, there will be no turning back." Lincoln caught the import of Grant's decision. "How near we have been to this thing before and failed," he exclaimed to his secretary. "I believe if any other general had been at the head of that army it would have been now on this side of the Rapidan."

Grant turned south after the Wilderness. Weeks and months of battle and siege lay ahead of him before he would achieve his objective of destroying Lee's army. But when he advanced instead of retiring, in that very action he had won the campaign. He refused to let Lee exercise a psychological ascendancy over him, as Lee had over every other Northern general, and he, having the initiative, now had an ascendancy over Lee. Many comparisons of the two great rivals have been made, and such evaluations are instructive. Lee was the better tactician and was more brilliant on the battlefield. Grant was the better strategist and had a broader view of the war. But in their dramatic meeting the decision came down to a question of will. It was a clash of two tremendous wills, two powerful characters. Grant triumphed, not because his will was any stronger than Lee's but because it was as strong and because he had the physical force to impose his will on his opponent. The campaign of 1864 is often treated in terms of numbers and supplies, and the result is attributed to purely material factors. All these played their part, but they would have been as nothing without the direction of a man.

There is no difficulty in composing a final evaluation of Ulysses S. Grant. The summation can be as short as one of his own deceivingly simple statements. With him there need be no balancing and qualifying, no ifs and buts. He won battles and campaigns, and he struck the blow that won the war. No general could do what he did because of accident or luck or preponderance of numbers and weapons. He was a success because he was a complete general and a complete character. He was so complete that his countrymen have never been able to believe he was real.

A Note on Bibliography

THE LITERATURE on Civil War generalship is, like treatments of other aspects of the conflict, immense. It is also highly controversial. There is something about the subject of generals and their battles that tempts authors to advance opinions and evaluations, and Civil War authors have been freer than most with their judgments. The result is a wide variety of verdicts that may seem confusing to the beginning student or reader but that is a part of the charm this war has for so many people. Here is the one area of American scholarly study where argumentation is cherished and the view of the amateur is as respected as that of the professional. A great deal of the writing about Civil War generals is, however, too largely descriptive. That is, many of the accounts describe a particular general in detail and assign him a rating without ever going into much analysis of how he got to be the kind of general he was. The following notes indicate some of the books on generals and generalship that analyze as well as recount. The volumes listed are, of

111

course, only a part of the writings available, and a number of good periodical articles have not been included. Dates of publication designates original and, when necessary, later editions.

For McClellan, there are two modern biographies. They are excellent pieces of scholarship but are laudatory, in fact, almost lyrical in tone: H. J. Eckenrode and Bryan Conrad, *George B. McClellan: The Man Who Saved the Union* (1941) and Warren W. Hassler, Jr., *General George B. McClellan: Shield of the Union* (1957). An earlier critical account that unfortunately has been lost sight of is Peter S. Michie, *General McClellan* (1901). McClellan composed an elaborate justification of his career in *McClellan's Own Story* (1887); it reveals more than he could have possibly known and provides all the material needed for a personal analysis of the author. The latest historical evaluation of McClellan is to be found in general works. It is unfavorable and even devastating; Kenneth P. Williams, *Lincoln Finds a General* (5 vols., 1949-1959), especially vols. I and II; Bruce Catton, *Mr. Lincoln's Army* (1951); and T. Harry Williams, *Lincoln and His Generals* (1952). The verdict in these books accords with that in two older works: Sir Frederick Maurice, *Statesmen and Soldiers of the Civil War* (1926), and Colin R. Ballard, *The Military Genius of Abraham Lincoln* (1926, 1952).

The two standard biographies of Sherman are Lloyd Lewis, *Sherman: Fighting Prophet* (1932, 1958), and B. H. Liddell Hart, *Sherman: Soldier, Realist, American* (1929, 1958). Both have their virtues and their defects. The Lewis volume is full and colorful but tends to lose Sherman's generalship in the detail of the story. The Liddell Hart book is often acutely analytical but frequently uses Sherman to expound the British author's own strategic theories. A good description of Sherman's last campaign is John G. Barrett, *Sherman's March Through the Carolinas* (1956). The general recounted his career at length in two big, breezy volumes of reminiscence, *Memoirs of General W. T. Sherman* (1875, 1887; one-vol. edition, 1957). The second edition is fuller than the first, but neither tells us as much about the author as we would like to know. A brief and critical evaluation of Sherman appears in Alfred H. Burne, *Lee, Grant and Sherman* (1938).

112

A Note on Bibliography

Perhaps the first serious student to note Grant's greatness was an English writer, C. F. Atkinson, in *Grant's Campaign of 1864 and 1865* (1908). Another English writer, a soldier-scholar, who argued Grant's case, although sometimes too aggressively, was General J. F. C. Fuller, *The Generalship of Ulysses S. Grant* (1929, 1958). From the American side, A. L. Conger wrote a perceptive appreciation, *The Rise of U. S. Grant* (1931). For years these were practically the only commentators heard in Grant's favor, although he received good marks in the previously cited works of Ballard and Burne. Grant's own account, *Personal Memoirs of U. S. Grant* (2 vols., 1885-1886; one-vol. edition, 1952), was rarely cited. Written in the last years of his life, it is, although not particularly self-revealing, a superior reminiscence, containing unusually clear battle narratives. Then in the 1950's a Grant revival got under way. Lloyd Lewis planned a multivolumed work, of which only one volume, *Captain Sam Grant* (1950), was finished at the time of his death. The Lewis project is being brought to completion by Bruce Catton, who has added *Grant Moves South* (1960). Kenneth P. Williams and T. Harry Williams frankly evaluated Grant as a great general in their works on the Northern command system, as did Catton in his *A Stillness at Appomattox* (1953). Edward Steere came to the same conclusion in his study of Grant in his most decisive test, *The Wilderness Campaign* (1960). Valuable material on Grant, and also on Sherman, appears in Francis F. McKinney's life of George H. Thomas, *Education in Violence* (1961), which represents a view not as yet accepted that Thomas deserves to rank with Grant and Sherman as the greatest of the Northern generals.

ELEPHANT PAPERBACKS

American History and American Studies

Stephen Vincent Benét, *John Brown's Body*, EL10
Paul Boyer, ed., *Reagan as President*, EL117
Robert V. Bruce, *1877: Year of Violence*, EL102
George Dangerfield, *The Era of Good Feelings*, EL110
Clarence Darrow, *Verdicts Out of Court*, EL2
Floyd Dell, *Intellectual Vagabondage*, EL13
Elisha P. Douglass, *Rebels and Democrats*, EL108
Theodore Draper, *The Roots of American Communism*, EL105
Joseph Epstein, *Ambition*, EL7
Paul W. Glad, *McKinley, Bryan, and the People*, EL119
Edward Chase Kirkland, *Dream and Thought in the Business
     Community, 1860–1900*, EL114
Herbert S Klein, *Slavery in the Americas*, EL103
Aileen S. Kraditor, *Means and Ends in American Abolitionism*,
     EL111
Leonard W. Levy, *Jefferson and Civil Liberties: The Darker Side*,
     EL107
Seymour J. Mandelbaum, *Boss Tweed's New York*, EL112
Thomas J. McCormick, *China Market*, EL115
Walter Millis, *The Martial Spirit*, EL104
Nicolaus Mills, ed., *Culture in an Age of Money*, EL302
Roderick Nash, *The Nervous Generation*, EL113
William L. O'Neill, ed., *Echoes of Revolt: The Masses,
     1911–1917*, EL5
Glenn Porter and Harold C. Livesay, *Merchants and
     Manufacturers*, EL106
Bernard Sternsher, ed., *Hitting Home: The Great Depression in
     Town and Country*, EL109
Nicholas von Hoffman, *We Are the People Our Parents Warned
     Us Against*, EL301
Norman Ware, *The Industrial Worker, 1840–1860*, EL116
Tom Wicker, *JFK and LBJ: The Influence of Personality upon
     Politics*, EL120
Robert H. Wiebe, *Businessmen and Reform*, EL101
T. Harry Williams, *McClellan, Sherman and Grant*, EL121
Miles Wolff, *Lunch at the 5 & 10*, EL118